Fairy Tales on Stage

A Collection of Children's Plays based on Fairy Tales

Julie Meighan

First published in 2016 by

JemBooks

Cork,

Ireland

http://drama-in-ecce.com

ISBN: 978-0-9568966-7-4

About the Author

Julie Meighan is a lecturer in Drama in Education at the Cork Institute of Technology. She has taught Drama to all age groups and levels. She is the author of the Amazon bestselling *Drama Start: Drama Activities, Plays and Monologues for Young Children (Ages 3 -8)* ISBN 978-0956896605, *Drama Start Two: Drama Activities and Plays for Children (Ages 9 -12)* ISBN 978-0-9568966-1-2 and *Stage Start: 20 Plays for Children (Ages 3-12)* ISBN 978-0956896629.

Julie Meighan

Table of Contents

About the Author i

Table Of Contents ii

Introduction 1

Drama Activities 2

 Warm-Up Games 2

 Character Development Games 6

 Group Work Games 11

 Concentration Games 14

 Imagination Games 18

Plays 21

 Little Red Riding Hood 21

 Goldilocks 26

 The Three Little Pigs 30

 The Elves and the Shoemaker 34

 The Three Billy Goats Gruff 38

 The Ugly Duckling 41

 The Lazy Cow 46

 The Talking Tree 49

 Humpty Dumpty 53

The Magic Porridge Pot   56

The Stone Soup   60

The Pied Piper of Hamelin   65

The Little Red Hen   69

The Gingerbread Man   74

The Enormous Turnip   78

Chicken Licken   81

Introduction

This book is a collection of plays that have been adapted from well-known fairy tales. They can be used as performance plays, readers theatre or just used to promote reading in groups. Each play is between five and ten minutes long. The plays can be adapted to suit the various needs of the group. The cast list is very flexible and characters can be added, changed or omitted. In addition, the teacher/group leader can assume the role of the storyteller if the children are unable to read or not at the reading level required. Also included in this book is a variety of drama activities. These activities are designed to be fun and enjoyable as well as promote coordination, movement, character development and creativity.

Props/costume/stage directions:

There is a minimal amount of props needed for these plays. Costumes can be very simple. The children can just wear clothes that are the same colour as their animal or their character. They can wear a mask or use some face paint. All suggestions for stage directions are included in brackets and italics.

Drama Activities

Warm-Up Games

Game: Imagine you are......

Age: 3 years +

Minimum number of participants: 1

Resources: Clear space.

Other Benefits: This game also stimulates the children's imagination and creativity.

Instructions: This game helps children do traditional stretches in a creative and fun way. These stretches can be done individually or in pairs.

Imagine you are a whisk

Get the children to put their hands over their heads and join their hands together and move their hands around in a large circle. First, get them to move their hands clockwise and when they are comfortable, get them to move their hands counter clockwise.

Imagine you are an inchworm

Get the children to bend down and put their hands on the ground. Next, get them to walk their hands out in front of them until they are supporting their body weight. They get into a push up position. Walk feet up to hands. Continue walking hands out and feet up to hands around the room. Make sure that they have their own space and don't bump into one another.

Imagine you are a car wiper

Get the children to lie on the ground. When they are comfortable, get them to put their legs in the air and then slowly move both legs from one side to another.

Imagine you are a cat stretching

Hands and feet are on the floor; arch back high in the air and stretch.

Imagine you are a giant

Get the children to take a big step and lunge on each step.

Imagine you are a marching soldier

Get the children to swing arms and bring legs up to the chest on each step.

Imagine you are a leaping frog

Get the children to squat down. They put their hands between their knees and jump around the space.

Game: Magic Bouncing Balls

Age: 4 years+

Minimum number of participants: 4

Resources: Clear space, a wand.

Other Benefits: This is also a very effective imagination game.

Instructions: Get each child to find a space. They must make sure they are not in anybody else's space. The teacher explains that the children are magic bouncing balls and she is a wizard with special powers. When she waves her magic wand, she can change them into anything she wants. If she says, "Magic bouncing balls, turn into roaring lions," they must all turn into roaring lions. Then she can say, "Magic bouncing balls, turn into magic bouncing balls," and they all bounce up and down in their own space again. The magic wizard can change the balls into anything she wants.

Suggestions:

Television

Rocking chair

Monster

Fish

Dog

Runner

Tree

Ballerina

Table

Lion

Mouse

Giant

Game: Pass the Hat

Age: 3 years+

Minimum number of participants: 3

Requirements: Clear space and a hat.

Other Benefits: This game also works well as a getting-to-know-you exercise.

Instructions: The children sit in a circle and the teacher gives one of the children a hat. Everyone chants "Child A has the hat. What do you think of that? Take it off and pass it to Child B." Child A takes the hat off slowly and passes to Child B. The children continue with the chant until everyone has had a turn. The last child takes off the hat and puts it away safely.

Character Development Games

Game: Object Freeze

Age: 3 years+

Minimum number of participants: 4

Requirements: Clear space, lively music, CD, child.

Other Benefits: This game also develops children's listening and concentration skills.

Instructions: The children free dance to some lively music. When the music stops, the teacher calls out an object and the children have to freeze in the shape of that object. If they move, they are out. The eliminated children get a chance to call out the object. You can use a theme. The following are some examples of different themes that could be used.

Halloween freeze:

Witch on her flying broomstick

Bat flying in the night

Zombie

Frightened child

Ghost

Frankenstein

Dracula

Bobbling apple

Pumpkin

Cat

Superhero freeze:

Superman/Super Girl

Batman/Batgirl

Wonder Woman

Iron Man

Aqua Man

Wolverine

The Hulk

Flash

Silver Surfer

Thor

Circus freeze:

Ring Master

Clown

Juggler

Knife Thrower

Elephants

Lion Tamer

Lions

Bears

Magician

Strongman

Game: Barnyard Walk

Age: 3 years+

Minimum number of participants: 4

Resources: Clear space.

Other Benefits: This activity promotes imagination and creativity.

Instructions: Encourage children to imitate different animals.

Horse - gallop and neigh

Pig- roll on the floor (in the mud) and oink

Duck - waddle and quack

Rooster - pretend to fly and crow

Cow - moo and walk slowly

Game: Crossing the Circle

Age: 4 years+

Minimum number of participants: 6

Resources: Clear space.

Other Benefits: This game is also very useful for developing listening and observation skills.

Instructions: Get the children to stand in a circle. The teacher gives each child a number: 1. 2 or 3. The teacher calls out a number, for example 3. Everyone in the circle who has the number 3 must cross the circle and swap places with someone else who has the same number. Once they have got used to crossing the circle, the teacher calls out a number as well as a way of moving.

Suggestions for ways of moving:

Stroll

Wander

March

Limp

Stagger

Crawl

Tiptoe

Stumble

Skip

If the children do not know the word (e.g., stagger), the teacher can explain what it means and demonstrate the movement. This is also a good game for expanding vocabulary.

Group Work Games

Game: Human Knot

Age: 6 years+

Minimum number of participants: 8

Resources: Clear space.

Other Benefits: This is an excellent movement and imagination game.

Instructions: Children form a close circle. Each child grabs different hands across the circle, forming a tangle of arms. It is best if children grab different hands. Then, they must untangle the knot (without letting go of each other's hands) by moving arms over heads or stepping over arms. Sometimes, the untangled knot will form two circles, and sometimes it will be impossible to untangle, but most of the time, the group will manage to untangle themselves.

Game: Dodge Ball

Age: 4 years+

Minimum number of participants: 4

Resources: A large soft ball.

Other Benefits: This is also an excellent warm-up game as well as helping children focus on what is happening around them.

Instructions: One child in the group is chosen to be "on." The child who is on has to throw a ball to hit the other children below the knee in order to catch them; The child who is on cannot run with the ball but once s/he has succeeded in hitting one of the others, they both become on and can pass the ball between them, making the game more difficult for the other children. While the children can dodge the ball by jumping and running, they cannot throw it. Only the children that have been caught can throw the ball

Game: Balloon Race Divide

Age: 4+

Minimum number of participants: 8

Resources: A balloon for each group and a clear space.

Other Benefits: This activity is useful to practice coordination.

Instructions: Divide the group into teams. There should be at least four children on each team. Each child stands behind one another. The child at the start of each line is given a balloon. The teacher calls out a part of the body and the children have to pass the balloon down the line just using that body part.

List of body parts that can be used:

Head

Arms

Shoulders

Hands

Fingers

Feet

Variation: Other dimensions could be included, such as pass the balloon standing on one leg, sitting down, without making eye contact.

Concentration Games

Game: Move, Move Pass It On

Age: 3 years+

Minimum number of participants: 4

Resources: Clear space.

Other Benefits: This game could also be used for imagination and gross motor skills.

Instructions: Everyone sits in a circle. The teacher teaches the group a song.

"Move, move, pass it on.

Move, move, pass it on.

Move, move pass it on.

Pass it around the circle."

The words of the song are sung to the tune of "Skip to My Lou."

Once they are comfortable with the song, the teacher makes a simple movement, such as putting her hands on her head or folding her arms. She passes on the movement to the child on her left. The child passes on the movement to the child next to them until the move is passed around the circle. While the movement is being passed around, everyone is singing the song. Everyone should get a chance to pass on a movement, but just make sure every movement is different.

Variation: You could also replace the word "move" with "squeeze" or "clap" to simplify the game.

Game: 1 to 10

Age: 5 years +

Minimum number of participants: 8

Resources: Clear space.

Other Benefits: This game is also useful for turn taking and teamwork.

Instructions: The children sit in a circle. They count from 1 to 10 together. Then they count from 10 to 1. They try to count from 1 to 10 working as a group. They jump up when they say the number. Anyone can say the number, but if two children say a number at the same time, then the group must start from the beginning. When they have mastered 1 to 10, then they try to count in reverse from 10 to 1. To make this more difficult, they can try to say the alphabet.

Game: String Shapes

Age: 4 years +

Minimum number of participants: 4

Resources: Clear space, a long piece of string for each group of four, blindfolds (optional).

Other Benefits: This activity can practice different types of shapes and promote imagination and group cohesion.

Instructions: Divide the group into smaller groups of 4. Give each group a long piece of string. Each member of the group is blindfolded or closes their eyes tightly. The teacher calls out a shape, such as square. Each group has to try to work together to make that shape with the string. The teacher gives them 30 seconds to complete the task. When the 30 seconds are up, then the groups stop and open their eyes. The teacher decides which group has made the best shaped square with their string and awards them a point. The group at the end with the most points, wins.

Shape suggestions:

Basic shapes

Circle

Square

Rectangle

Triangle

Oval

Advanced shapes

Trapezoid

Parallelogram

Pentagon

Hexagon

Octagon

Diamond

Star

Heart

Arrow

Crescent

Cube

Imagination Games

Game: The Night at the Museum

Age: 4 years +

Minimum number of participants: 4

Resources: Clear space.

Other Benefits: This activity will also stimulate the children's imagination.

Instructions: The teacher/facilitator or one of the children volunteers to be a security guard. All the children spread out and become a selected museum artefact. They become a sculpt of their chosen artefact. The security guard walks around the space. When his/her back is turned, the children change position. If the children are seen, they are removed from the display floor. The last child left becomes the new security guard.

Suggestion of different types of museums:

Waxworks

Prehistoric

Art

Dinosaur

Science

Music hall of fame

Game: What can you do with a Piece of String?

Age: 4 years+

Minimum number of participants: 4

Resources: Clear space and a piece of sting for each team.

Other Benefits: This activity gives the children an opportunity to use their creativity and imagination.

Instructions: Divide the groups into small groups of 4. Give each group a piece of string. Give them 3 minutes to come up with as many things they can turn the piece of string into. For example, it could be a tightrope, a swimming pool, a rope in a tug of war, etc. At the end of the 3 minutes, the groups must show the rest of the class the items that they turned their string into and use them. Each group gets a point for each original use of the string. The winner is the group with the most points.

Game: Transport

Age: 4 years+

Minimum number of participants: 2

Resources: Pictures of different types of transport, clear space and a licence for each child.

Other Benefits: This is a very good movement game.

Instructions: The children sit in a circle and the teacher shows them pictures of different modes of transportation. They discuss how the different modes of transportation move. Each child has to choose to be a different mode of transportation. The teacher tells the children to find their own space and that they are going to move around like their chosen method of transportation. Make sure they understand the rules of the road. They can't bump into anyone else and if they do, their licence will be taken from them and they will be banned from the game for 1 minute. Tell them to turn on their engine and rev it up. Then they move like their particular mode of transportation. The teacher will call out different ways of moving.

Suggested ways of moving:

Reverse

Go over speed bumps fast

Go uphill slowly

Go downhill

Make a sharp turn

Make an emergency stop

Avoid an oncoming speeding car

Go fast but slow down at speeding lights

Come to a complete stop at a red light

Plays

Little Red Riding Hood

Characters: Three storytellers. Red Riding Hood, wolf, grandma, Red Riding Hood's mother, woodcutter, trees.

Storyteller 1: Once upon a time there lived a little girl called little Red Riding Hood.

Storyteller 2: She was called Red Riding Hood because she always wore a cape with a red hood.

Storyteller 3: She was a very helpful little girl. One day her mother said...

Mother: Your grandmother is very ill. Take this basket of food and visit her. She would love to see you.

Red Riding Hood: Thank you, Mother. *(She takes the basket and off she goes to see her grandmother.)*

(Trees are scattered all over the stage.)

Tree 1: Look, there is a little girl walking in the forest by herself.

Tree 2: Do you think we should tell her it is dangerous?

Tree 3: She should know the Big Bad Wolf is always sniffing around.

Tree 1: The Big Bad Wolf is very nasty.

Tree 2: And scary.

Tree 3: He will eat anything.

Tree 1: I think we should tell her.

Tree 2: It is too late.

Tree 3: Here comes the Big Bad Wolf. *(Big Bad wolf enters.)*

Wolf: Hello, Red Riding Hood. Where are you off to on this lovely, fine day?

Red Riding Hood: I'm going to visit my grandmother. She is very sick and I am going to bring her some food and these lovely flowers.

Wolf: But you are going the long way. *(He points to the opposite direction.)* That way is shorter.

Red Riding Hood: Oh thank you, Mr. Wolf. *(Off she goes in the wrong direction.)*

(Wolf laughs loudly and runs off stage in the opposite direction.)

Tree 1: He told Red Riding Hood to go to her grandmother's house the long way.

Tree 2: He is up to something.

Tree 3: Something very bad.

(Grandmother comes on stage. She is sitting in a chair. She looks very sick. The wolf arrives.)

Wolf: Knock, knock.

Grandmother: Who is it?

Wolf: Red Riding Hood.

Grandmother: Come in, my dear. *(Wolf walks in and grandmother gets a fright.)*

Grandmother: You are not Red Riding Hood. *(She jumps up and starts to run around the room. The wolf chases her. Then there is a knock on the door. The wolf grabs grandmother and puts her in the closet. He puts on her hat and glasses and gets into the chair.)*

Red Riding Hood: Knock, knock.

Wolf: Come in, Red Riding Hood.

Red Riding Hood: I've brought some nice food to help you get better.

Wolf: Why thank you, my dear.

Red Riding Hood: *(looks at grandmother)* Why grandmother, what big eyes you have!

Wolf: All the better to see you with, my dear.

Red Riding Hood: Why grandmother, what big ears you have!

Wolf: All the better to hear you with, my dear.

Red Riding Hood: Why grandmother, what big teeth you have!

Wolf: All the better to eat you with, my dear.

(The wolf jumps up and runs after Red Riding Hood. He chases her around the room.)

Tree 1: Do you hear screams?

Tree 2: We should call the woodsman to help.

Tree 3: Let's all shout for help together.

Trees: Woodsman, help, help!

(Woodsman comes racing in.)

Woodsman: What is all the noise about?

Tree 1: The Big Bad Wolf is in the grandmother's house.

Tree 2: He is chasing Red Riding Hood. He wants to eat her.

Tree 3: You need to save her.

(Woodsman runs into the house and grabs the wolf.)

Woodsman: What do you think you are doing? *(He waves the axe at him and chases him out of the house and off the stage.)*

Wolf: *(screams)* AARRGHHHHH!

Woodsman: And don't come back ever.

(Red Riding Hood gets her grandmother from the closet. They hug.)

Grandmother/Red Riding Hood: Thank you, Woodsman

Grandmother: Would you like to stay for tea?

Woodsman: Oh yes, please.

Storyteller 1: They all sat down and enjoyed their tea.

Storyteller 2: The lesson of the story is...

Storyteller 3: Don't talk to strangers.

Goldilocks

Characters: Three storytellers, Goldilocks, three bears, three bowls, three chairs, three beds.

Storyteller 1: Once upon a time, there were three bears who lived in a little house in the woods.

Storyteller 2: There was Daddy Bear, there was Mummy Bear and there was Baby Bear.

Storyteller 3: One fine day, they decided to go for a walk.

Daddy Bear: What a lovely sunny day it is today. Let's all go to the woods.

Baby Bear: I'm hungry. I want to eat my porridge.

Mummy Bear: The porridge is still hot; it will be cool enough by the time we come back from our walk.

Storyteller 1: So, off they went on their walk.

Storyteller 2: Just then, a little girl called Goldilocks was walking in the woods.

Storyteller 3: She was picking flowers for her grandma.

Storyteller 1: She stopped suddenly and saw a pretty little house.

Goldilocks: Oh, what a pretty little house. I am feeling a little tired and hungry. I wonder if whoever lives here will let me rest for a few moments and give me something to eat *(She knocks on the door.)* There is no answer.... (*She opens the door slowly and goes inside.*)

26

Goldilocks: Oh look, three bowls of porridge.

Bowl 1: Eat me! I have lots of salt on me. (*Goldilocks eats some but spits it out.*)

Goldilocks: Yuck! You are too salty.

Bowl 2: I have lots of sugar on me. (*Goldilocks eats some but spits it out.*)

Goldilocks: Yuck! You are too sugary.

Bowl 3: Eat me! I'm just right. (*Goldilocks eats some and likes it and continues eating it until all the porridge is gone.*)

Goldilocks: Mmmmmm, that was just right. Oh look, three chairs. I think I'll sit down for a moment.

Chair 1: Sit on me. I'm very hard. (*Goldilocks goes to sit down and jumps up straight away.*)

Goldilocks: This chair is too hard.

Chair 2: Sit on me. I'm very soft. (*Goldilocks goes to sit down and jumps up straight away.*)

Goldilocks: This chair is too soft.

Chair 3: Sit on me. I'm just right. (*Goldilocks goes to sit down and makes herself comfortable.*)

Goldilocks: This chair is just right. Oh dear, I've broken the chair.

Storyteller 2: Goldilocks decided to walk upstairs.

Storyteller 3: She saw three beds.

Bed 1: Lie on me. I'm very hard. *(Goldilocks lies down on the bed and suddenly jumps up.)*

Goldilocks: This bed is too hard.

Bed 2: Lie on me. I'm very soft. *(Goldilocks lies down on the bed and suddenly jumps up.)*

Goldilocks: This bed is too soft.

Bed 3: Lie on me. I'm just right. *(Goldilocks lies down on the bed and stays there.)*

Goldilocks: This bed is just right.

Storyteller 1: Goldilocks fell fast asleep.

Storyteller 2: After a while, the three bears came back from their walk.

Storyteller 3: They walked in to the house and Daddy Bear said...

Daddy Bear: Who has been eating my porridge?

Storyteller 1: Mummy Bear said...

Mummy Bear: Who has been eating my porridge?

Storyteller 2: Baby Bear said...

Baby Bear: Who has been eating my porridge? Look, it is all gone!

Storyteller 3: They saw the chairs and Daddy Bear said...

Daddy Bear: Who has been sitting on my chair?

Storyteller 2: Mummy Bear said...

Mummy Bear: Who has been sitting on my chair?

Storyteller 2: Baby Bear said...

Baby Bear: Who has been sitting on my chair? Look, it's broken!

Storyteller 3: They walked upstairs and Daddy Bear said...

Daddy Bear: Who has been sleeping in my bed?

Storyteller 1: Mummy Bear said...

Mummy Bear: Who has been sleeping in my bed?

Storyteller 2: Baby Bear said...

Baby Bear: Who has been sleeping in my bed? And look, she is still there!

Storyteller 3: Goldilocks woke and screamed.

Storyteller 1: She jumped out of bed and ran down the stairs and out of the house.

Storyteller 2: The three bears never saw her again

Storytellers: The end.

The Three Little Pigs

Characters: First Little Pig, Second Little Pig, Third Little Pig, Mother, Man with Straw, Man with Sticks, Man with Bricks, Big Bad Wolf, and three storytellers.

Storyteller 1: Once upon a time, there lived three little pigs.

Storyteller 2: They lived at home with their mother.

Storyteller 3: One day, their mother said...

Mother: You are old enough to go out into the world and make it on your own.

Storyteller 1: She gave them some food and said goodbye. *(She gives them some food and they all hug her.)*

Mother: Bye, bye. *(She waves goodbye.)*

Little Pigs: Bye, Mother. *(They wave at their mother.)*

First Little Pig: It's so exciting to be out in the world by ourselves. *(A man with straw passes by.)*

First Little Pig: Please, sir, may I have some straw so I can build a house of my very own?

Man with Straw: Certainly; here you go. *(Man gives the First Little Pig straw and he starts to build his house.)*

Storyteller 2: The other two pigs said goodbye and continued on their way. *(They all hug each other and they wave goodbye.)*

Second Little Pig: It's so exciting to be out in the world by ourselves. (*A man with sticks passes by.*)

Second Little Pig: Please, sir, may I have some sticks so I can build a house of my very own?

Man with Sticks: Certainly; here you go. (*Man gives the Second Little Pig sticks and he starts to build his house.*)

Storyteller 3: The Third Little Pig said goodbye and continued on his way. (*He hugs his brother and goes on his way.*)

Third Little Pig: It's so exciting to be out in the world by myself. (*A man with bricks passes by.*)

Third Little Pig: Please, sir, may I have some bricks so I can build a house of my very own?

Man with Bricks: Certainly; here you go. (*Man gives the Third Little Pig bricks and he starts to build his house.*)

Storyteller 1: The Third Little Pig made his house of bricks.

Storyteller 2: One day, a big, bad wolf came knocking at the first little pig's house.

Big Bad Wolf: (*Knocks*) Little pig, little pig, let me come in!

First Little Pig: Not by the hair of my chinny-chin-chin.

Big Bad Wolf: Then I will huff and I will puff and I will blow your house down.

Storyteller 3: So he huffed and he puffed and he blew the house down. (*The First Little Pig ran to his brother's house made of sticks.*)

First Little Pig: Help, help, the wolf is after me!

Second Little Pig: Come in and sit down; you will be safe here. (*He gives him a cup of tea.*)

Storyteller 1: One day, a big, bad wolf came knocking on the Second Little Pig's house.

Big Bad Wolf: (*knocks*) Little pig, little pig, let me come in.

Second Little Pig: Not by the hair of my chinny-chin-chin.

Big Bad Wolf: Then I will huff and I will puff and I will blow your house down.

Storyteller 2: So he huffed and he puffed and he blew the house down. (*The First and the Second Little Pigs run to their brother's house made of bricks.*)

First Little Pig/Second Little Pig: Help, help, the wolf is after us!

Third Little Pig: Come in and sit down; you will be safe here. (*He gives them cups of tea.*)

Storyteller 3: A few days later, the wolf came knocking on the Third Little Pig's door.

Big Bad Wolf: (*knocks*) Little pig, little pig, let me come in.

First Little Pig: Not by the hair of my chinny-chin-chin.

Big Bad Wolf: Then I will huff and I will puff and I will blow your house down.

Storyteller 1: So he huffed and he puffed and huffed and he puffed and he huffed and he puffed but he couldn't blow the house down.

Storyteller 2: So, he decided to climb up on the roof. (*The wolf mimes climbing up on the roof.*)

First Little Pig: Did you hear that?

Second Little Pig: What?

Third Little Pig: Sssssssssh, It's the wolf on the roof. I've an idea. Put some water to boil on the fire. (*They mime putting a pot of boiling water on the fire.*)

Big Bad Wolf: Little pigs, I am coming to get you. Ohhh!

(*Big Bad Wolf falls into the boiling water and runs out of the house screaming in pain. Three Little Pigs are laughing.*)

Pigs: Ha! Ha!

Storyteller 3: And the Three Little Pigs lived happily ever after

The Elves and the Shoemaker

Characters: Shoemaker, his wife, three customers, three narrators, and four elves.

Narrator 1: There once lived a shoemaker who was very kind but very poor.

Narrator 2: He and his wife had nothing to eat. *(The Shoemaker and his wife are centre stage; the shoemaker is looking at some leather he has and the wife is looking around the kitchen for some food.)*

Shoemaker: I'm so hungry! I have only got this one piece of leather left. *(He holds ups the leather.)* I will leave it here and make the shoes in the morning.

Wife: Let's go to bed. *(They go to the side of the stage and go to sleep.)*

Narrator 3: The next morning, the shoemaker woke up and came downstairs.

Narrator 1: On his table were the most beautiful shoes he had ever seen.

Shoemaker: *(Looks admiringly at the shoes.)* Am I dreaming?

Wife: *(Shocked.)* Who made these marvellous shoes?

(A customer walks into the shop, so they stop talking, smile and greet her.)

Customer 1: Oh my, what beautiful shoes! I must have them. Here, keep the change. (*She gives the shoemaker money and exits the shop.*)

Shoemaker: Look, we have enough money to buy leather for two pairs of shoes and some food. (*The shoemaker and his wife hug each other and jump up and down with excitement.*)

Narrator 2: The next day, the shoemaker and his wife woke up and found two pairs of shoes. They were more beautiful than the first pair.

Wife: Oh, what beautiful shoes. Who is making them?

Shoemaker: I don't know.

Customer 2: (*Enters.*) I just saw those shoes in the window. Can I buy them?

Shoemaker: Certainly. (*Gives her the shoes.*)

Customer 2: Keep the change. (*Exits the shop.*)

(*Customer 3 enters, very excited.*)

Customer 3: I just saw the most beautiful shoes in the window. Can I buy them?

Shoemaker: Certainly. (*Gives her the second pair of shoes.*)

Customer 3: Keep the change. (*Exits the shop.*)

Shoemaker: (*Looks at money.*) Now I've enough money to buy four pieces of leather.

Narrator 3: Over the next few weeks, the shoe shop became very popular.

Narrator 1: The shoemaker and his wife went to bed every night.

Narrator 2: And every morning there were always new shoes waiting to be sold.

Shoemaker: I can't work it out. What kind of magic is making all these beautiful shoes? I've a plan. (*He whispers to his wife. Both of them whisper to each other. The audience can't hear.*)

Narrator 3: So that night, instead of going to bed like they usually did, they hid behind the table.

Narrator 1: When the clock struck midnight, four elves came in tiptoeing into the room.

Elf 1: Look, he has left more leather.

Elf 2: Let's make some shoes for the kind old man and his wife.

Elf 3: They will be so happy when they see these beautiful shoes.

Elf 4: Come, it's time to leave; be quiet everyone. (*They tiptoe quietly and slowly and exit the stage. Shoemaker and his wife come out from behind the table.*)

Wife: They have made us rich.

Shoemaker: We have to return the favour, and I've a plan. (*He whispers in his wife's ear and she nods her head.*)

Narrator 1: So the old man and his wife worked all day to make the elves little green suits and shoes.

Narrator 2: When the clock struck midnight, the shoemaker and his wife hid behind the table again and waited. *(The elves tiptoe in the room very quietly.)*

Elf 1: Sssshhh!

Elf 2: Look at these. *(Holds up the elves' suits and shoes.)*

Elf 3: This is the most beautiful present anyone has ever given us.

Elf 4: Let's put them on. *(They admire themselves and jump up and down with excitement.)*

Narrator 3: The old man and his wife never saw the elves again.

Narrator 1: But they never went hungry again because they were so rich from selling shoes that they never had to work again.

The Three Billy Goats Gruff

Characters: Three storytellers, the Smallest Billy Goat, the Middle-sized Billy Goat and the Biggest Billy Goat and the troll.

(Stage directions: The three billy goats are happily playing with each other and the three storytellers are on the left side of the stage.)

Storyteller 1: Once upon a time, there lived three billy goats gruff.

Storyteller 2: They spent every winter in a barn that kept them nice and warm.

Storyteller 3: But when the summer came, they liked to trippety trip over the bridge to the beautiful green meadow on the other side of the river.

Smallest Billy Goat: I'm really hungry. I think I will cross the bridge to eat some lovely green grass in the meadow.

Storyteller 1: What the billy goats didn't know was that under the bridge, there lived a really ugly troll.

Storyteller 2: The troll was nasty and horrible.

Storyteller 3: Nobody crossed the bridge without the troll's permission and he never gave permission.

Smallest Billy Goat: I can't wait to get to the meadow. *(He goes trippety tripping on the bridge, but halfway over, out pops the troll.)*

Troll: Who is that trippety tripping over my bridge?

Smallest Billy Goat: Oh, it's only me. Please let me pass. I only want to go to the meadow to eat some sweet grass.

Troll: Oh no you are not. I'm going to eat you.

Smallest Billy Goat: Oh, no, please, Mr. Troll, I'm only the smallest Billy Goat Gruff. I'm much too tiny for you to eat, and I wouldn't taste very good. Why don t you wait for my brother, the middle-sized billy goat? He is much bigger than I am and would be much tastier.

Troll: Well, I suppose I could wait.

Middle-Sized Billy Goat: I think I will join my brother on the meadow and eat some lovely lush grass. *(He goes trippety tripping on the bridge, but halfway over, out pops the troll.)*

Troll: Who is that trippety tripping over my bridge?

Smallest Billy Goat: Oh it's only me. Please let me pass. I only want to go to the meadow to eat some sweet grass.

Troll: Oh no, you are not. I'm going to eat you.

Middle-Sized Billy Goat: Oh, no, please, Mr. Troll, I'm only the middle-sized Billy Goat Gruff. I'm much too tiny for you to eat, and I wouldn't taste very good. Why don t you wait for my brother, the third billy goat? He is much bigger than I am and would be much tastier.

Troll: Well, I suppose I could wait.

Biggest Billy Goat: I am all alone here; I think I will join my brothers in the meadow and get some nice sweet grass to eat.

(He goes trippety tripping on the bridge, but halfway over, out pops the troll.)

Troll: Who is that trippety tripping over my bridge?

Biggest Billy Goat: Oh it only me. Please let me pass. I only want to go to the meadow to eat some sweet grass.

Troll: Oh no you are not. I'm going to eat you.

Biggest Billy Goat: That's what you think!

Storyteller 1: He lowered his horns, galloped along the bridge and butted the ugly troll. Up, up, up, went the troll into the air...

Storyteller 2: Then down, down, down into the rushing river below. He disappeared below the swirling waters.

Biggest Billy Goat: That taught him a lesson.

Storyteller 3: He continued across the bridge and met with his brothers and they ate grass and played for the rest of summer. *(The three billy goats play with each other.)*

The Ugly Duckling

Characters: Three storytellers, the Ugly Duckling, Mother Duck, Old Duck, ducklings, four ducks, turkey, red hen, chickens, two dogs, two wild ducks, tom cat, two children.

(Stage directions: Storytellers on the left-hand side of the stage and the mother duck in the centre sitting on her eggs. Eggs could be painted balloons that burst as soon as the eggs crack.)

Storyteller 1: There was once duck that lived near a deep river.

Storyteller 2: The duck was sitting on her eggs in her nest...

Storyteller 3: Waiting for the eggs to hatch.

Storyteller 1: She had been there a long time.

Storyteller 2: She was starting to get bored.

Mother Duck: I have been sitting on my eggs for such a long time. *(Mother Duck sighs loudly.)*

Storyteller 1: Suddenly, she heard a noise. *(Children can make a cracking noise from behind or off stage.)*

Mother Duck: What was that? Oh my goodness, the eggs are beginning to hatch at last. *(She looks at the eggs with a shocked look on her face.)*

Storyteller 2: One shell cracked, then another. *(Cracking noises come from off stage and then each duck lifts their head and says* peep, peep *and* quack, quack.*)*

Old Duck: *(Old Duck enters the stage while Mother Duck is playing with the ducklings.)* Have all your eggs hatched, Mother Duck?

Mother Duck: One egg has not hatched, but just look at all the others. Aren't they the prettiest little ducklings you ever saw? *(They all stare at the egg that hasn't hatched.)*

Mother Duck: I will have to sit on it for a while longer. *(She goes back to sitting on her nest.)*

Old Duck: Please yourself. *(Old Duck leaves the stage.)*

Storyteller 1: At last, the egg hatched and out came the little duckling. *(He says* peep, peep *and* quack, quack *very loudly.)*

Storyteller 2: He wasn't that little.

Ugly Duckling: Peep peep, quack, quack.

Ducklings: *(They all point at him.)* Look at him! He's so big and he's very ugly.

Storyteller 3: All the other little ducklings pointed and laughed at him.

Storyteller 3: The next day...

Mother Duck: Follow me ducklings, I'm going to teach you to swim. *(They all follow Mother Duck in a row. The Ugly Duckling is last in the line.)*

Storyteller 1: They went to the river and they saw other ducks and they began to laugh at the ugly duckling.

Duck 1: Here comes another brood.

Duck 2: As if there aren't enough of us already.

Duck 3: That last duck sure is ugly.

Duck 4: We don't want him here.

(They surround him and start to poke him.)

Mother Duck: Let him alone. *(She pushes the other ducks off him.)* He was just in his egg too long and came out a little funny.

Storyteller 2: It wasn't just the ducks that made fun of him; the other animals did, too. *(The turkey and chickens all surround the ugly duckling.)*

Turkey: He is too big.

Chicken 1: He is so ugly.

Chickens: He looks scary *(Chicken 1 starts to peck him and leaves the stage; the ugly duckling starts to run and bumps into two wild ducks.)*

Storyteller 3: The little duck was so scared that he ran away.

Storyteller 1: Then he met two wild ducks.

Wild Duck 1: What kind of a duck are you?

Wild Duck 2: A really ugly one! *(They laugh and start to poke him.)*

(Dog starts chasing the wild ducks and they run away.)

Dog 1: What kind of a duck are you?

Dog 2: You are so ugly. *(The dogs run away looking scared.)*

Ugly Duckling: Even the dogs won't chase me as I'm really ugly.

Storyteller 2: He ran over the field and the meadow until he was cold and hungry.

Storyteller 2: He came to a little cottage. *(He knocks on the door and goes inside.)*

Storyteller 3: A tom cat and a little red hen lived in the cottage. *(They are sitting down by the fire.)*

Tom Cat: What do you want?

Ugly Duckling: I want somewhere to stay.

Red Hen: You can't stay here; you are too ugly.

Tom Cat: Be on your way. *(They shoo the ugly duckling away.)*

Storyteller 1: Summer turned into autumn and the leaves in the forest turned to orange.

Storyteller 2: Winter came and so did the wind, rain and snow.

Storyteller 3: The ugly duckling was exhausted and fell asleep on the frozen river.

Ugly Duckling: I am so sad. I've no family, friends and I'm so ugly no one wants to be friends with me. (*The ugly duckling cries and falls asleep.*)

Storyteller 1: Winter turned to spring and some children came to the lake and started to throw bread at the duck.

Child 1: Look at the swans; they are so beautiful.

Child 2: But the new one is the most beautiful of them all. He is so young and pretty. (*They point to the ugly duckling.*)

Ugly Duckling: Are they talking to me? (*He looks around and points to himself and he looks at his reflection in the water.*)

Ugly Duckling: I am beautiful! I never dreamed of such happiness as this while I was the ugly duckling.

The Lazy Cow

Characters: Three storytellers, the Lazy Cow, three cows, pigs, hens and owls.

(Stage Directions: the pigs, hens and dogs are in a large semicircle stage right; storytellers are stage left and the ants are in the centre of the stage.)

Storyteller 1: One hot summer's day...

Storyteller 2: There were some cows working hard.

Storyteller 3: They were collecting food for the winter. *(All the cows are miming digging, pulling and pushing.)*

Cow 1: I am so hot.

Cow 2: Me too!

Cow 3: This is very hard work.

Storyteller 1: They saw the Lazy Cow listening to some music on his iPod. *(Lazy Cow passes by, singing and dancing; the three cows stop work and look at him.)*

Storyteller 2: He was dancing.

Storyteller 3: And laughing and enjoying the lovely weather.

Lazy Cow: Cows, you are so silly. You need to enjoy the sunshine.

(Cows start working again.)

Cow 1: We are working hard.

Cow 2: We want to have food for the winter. *(The Lazy Cow keeps dancing.)*

Storyteller 1: The Lazy Cow continued enjoying himself. *(The cows keep working and move stage right.)*

Storyteller 2: Winter started to come, and the weather got colder and colder.

Storyteller 3: The snow began to fall.

Storyteller 1: The Lazy Cow was cold and hungry. *(He rubs his stomach and shivers. He looks at the owls that start to fly around the stage.)*

Lazy Cow: I am cold and hungry; perhaps my friends the owls will feed me. Owls! Owls! Will you please feed me?

Owls: *(Owls fly around the lazy cow and stop centre stage. They stand around the lazy cow.)* Twit Tuhooo! Oh no, we will not feed you. *(They fly back to their place in the semicircle.)*

The Lazy Cow: Oh dear! I know, I will ask my friends the pigs to feed me. *(Lazy Cow walks towards the pigs.)* Pigs! Pigs! Please feed me. *(Pigs are asleep, so he wakes them up and they walk to the centre stage.)*

Pigs: *(The pigs are very angry that they have been woken up.)* Oink, Oink, oh no, we will not feed you. *(The pigs go back to their place in the semicircle.)*

Storyteller 1: Then the lazy cow saw some hens. *(The hens mime eating grain stage right.)*

Lazy Cow: Hens! hens! Please feed me! *(They hens walk towards him.)*

Hens: Oh no, we will not feed you. *(They hop back to stage right.)*

Storyteller 2: The Lazy Cow was very cold and hungry. He didn't know what to do. *(The Lazy Cow is shivering and rubbing his stomach.)*

Storyteller 3: Then he thought of the other three cows. *(The three cows move to the centre of the stage.)*

Lazy Cow: Cows! Cows! Please feed me. *(The cows go into a huddle away from the Lazy Cow.)*

Storyteller 1: The cows thought about it and decided to give him some food. *(All the cows face the Lazy Cow.)*

Cow 1: You must promise that next year you will work hard in the summer. *(Lazy Cow gets down on his hands and knees.)*

Lazy Cow: Oh thank you, Cows, I promise.

Storyteller 1: That summer, the lazy cow kept his promise and worked hard to collect food for the next winter. *(Lazy Cow mimes pushing, pulling, carrying and digging with all other cows.)*

Storyteller 2: The lesson of the story is: Fail to prepare...

Storyteller 3: Prepare to fail.

The Talking Tree

Characters: Three storytellers, three gods, sun, wind, rain, monkey/s, lion/s, snake/s, fruit tree/s, blossom tree/s.

Storyteller 1: Once upon a time.

Storyteller 2: A long, long, time ago.

Storyteller 3: The gods made the world. *(Gods are elevated on boxes or chairs.)*

God 1: *(Waves magic wand.)* Here is some land.

God 2: But we need something to put on the land.

God 3: I know...how about some animals and plants?

God 1: What a fabulous idea.

Storyteller 1: They filled the land with all types of animals and plants and flowers.

God 2: Well done everyone, but I think we are missing something.

God 1 & 3: What?

God 2: A talking tree. *(They all wave their magic wands and a tree appears.)*

Talking Tree: Hello gods, thank you for making me.

Storyteller 2: At first, the gods were happy with their tree.

Storyteller 3: They sent rain when it was thirsty. *(Everyone claps to make the sound of the rain.)*

Rain: Here is some water to help you grow.

Storyteller 1: They sent him sun to keep him warm.

Sun: Here is some heat to keep you warm.

Storyteller 2: They sent him wind when it was too hot.

Wind: Here is a nice breeze to keep you cool.

(Talking Tree doesn't look happy.)

Talking Tree: *(To the rain)* This is too much; now I'm wet and cold. *(To the sun)* Now I'm too hot and *(to the wind)* I'm going to blow over. *(Monkey come in and start to climb the tree and eat his leaves.)*

Monkey: These leaves are delicious. You should grow some bananas on your branches. *(Tree shakes off the monkey. Lion comes in and looks at the tree.)*

Lion: This tree looks like a good place to sleep. *(The tree starts shaking his leaves and they fall on the lion.)*

(Snake comes in and looks at the tree.)

Snake: That tree will be a good thing to slither up. *(The snake starts slithering up the tree and the tree pushes him off.)*

Talking Tree: I'm sick of all these animals climbing on top of me and sleeping below me.

Storyteller 1: The tree always found something to complain about.

Storyteller 2: He moaned and groaned, but the gods got on with their world.

Storyteller 3: They made trees with blossoms and bright flowers. They made trees with different types of fruits on them. *(Different types of trees start to appear on the stage.)*

Talking Tree: Gods, why did you make me so plain?

God 1: That tree never stops complaining.

God 2: What shall we do?

God 3: I know. *(They all whisper together.)*

Gods: Stop moaning.

Talking Tree: Why should I?

Fruit Tree/s: We have such lovely fruit.

Talking Tree: I want fruit. Why can't I have fruit?

Blossom Tree/s: What lovely flowers we have.

Talking Tree: I want flowers. Why can't I have flowers?

Gods: Stop talking; we can't take all your moaning and groaning.

Talking Tree: Make me.

Storyteller 1: The gods grabbed him and turned him upside down.

Storyteller 2: The talking tree was completely silent for the first time ever.

Monkey: No more moaning and groaning

Lion: We don't have to listen to him anymore.

Snake: Silence at last.

Storyteller 3: From then on, no one ever heard from the talking tree again and they all lived happily ever after.

Humpty Dumpty

Characters: Humpty Dumpty, Egg 1, Egg 2, Egg 3, Egg 4, General, King's man 1, King's man 2, King's man 3, King's horse 1, King's horse 2, King's horse 3, King and Servant.

(Stage directions: There is a big wall upstage and there is a group of eggs playing outside the wall. They accidentally throw the ball over the wall.)

Egg 1: Oh dear, what will we do now?

Egg 2: Well, one of us will have to climb over the wall and get the ball.

Egg 3: Humpty Dumpty will do it.

Humpty Dumpty: Why do I have to do it?

Egg 4: Because you are bravest egg of all eggs.

Egg 1: Don't tell us you are scared.

All: Scaredy Egg! Scaredy Egg!

Humpty Dumpty: Alright, alright, I'll do it.

(Humpty Dumpty starts to climb the wall. He is shaking because he is so scared. He gets to the top, but he is too frightened to move.)

Humpty Dumpty: I can't move. What shall I do?

(Enters General.)

General: What is going on here?

(All the eggs run off.)

Humpty Dumpty: I climbed the wall because we threw the ball over the wall and I wanted to get it back for all my egg friends, but now I'm stuck and I can't get down.

General: I'll get a ladder and help you get down. *(General mimes getting a ladder but Humpty Dumpty starts to wobble and falls off the wall.)*

Humpty Dumpty: Help me! I'm broken. *(Humpty Dumpty is lying on the floor.)*

General: Don't worry, I'll call all the King's men to come and help put you back together again.

General: *(Gets out his phone and dials the King's men.)* Please, come quickly. A giant egg has fallen off a wall.

(King's men come galloping in on their horses. They look at Humpty Dumpty on the ground.)

King's Man 1: Oh dear, this looks very bad.

King's Horse 1: I don't think we are going to be able to fix him.

King's Man 2: Don't give up; we can try.

King's Horse 2: Look, everybody—where do you think this goes? *(He holds up an arm.)*

King's Man 3: I think that might be his leg. *(They all try hard to put him back together. They circle him so the audience can't see while they are working on him. Then after a few minutes, they stop.)*

King's Horse 3: We tried our best, but there is nothing we can do. (They all put their heads down.)

(Trumpet blows and the King's servant enters.)

Servant: The king is coming; everyone bow. *(They all bow as the King enters and sits at the table.)*

King: I'm so hungry. *(Rings bell)* What is for dinner tonight, servant?

Servant: Lots and lots of scrambled egg.

All: *(Come out to the centre stage and recite the Humpty Dumpty rhyme)*

Humpty Dumpty sat on a wall.

Humpty Dumpty had a great fall.

All the king's horses and all the king's men

Couldn't put Humpty together again.

They tried to push him up.

They tried to pull him up.

They tried to patch him up,

But couldn't put him back together again.

The Magic Porridge Pot

Characters: Two storytellers, Daisy, Maisy, Mother, four villagers, old woman and the porridge pot.

Storyteller 1: Once upon a time, there was a little girl called Daisy who lived with her mother in a very small house.

Storyteller 2: They were very poor and they didn't have much to eat. One day, they were really, really, really hungry.

Mother: I am very hungry. (*She rubs her tummy.*)

Daisy: I know, I will go into the forest and collect some mushrooms.

(*She walks into the forest by herself and starts collecting mushrooms. Suddenly, an old woman creeps up behind her.*)

Old Woman: What are you doing, little girl?

Daisy: My mother and I are very hungry. I am looking for some mushrooms for us to eat for our tea.

Old Woman: (*She hands the little girl a porridge pot.*) Here, take this.

Porridge Pot: Oh, dear, what is to become of me? (*Starts crying.*)

Old Woman: I am travelling far away and I can't take this porridge pot with me. *(Woman walks off.)*

Daisy: (Looks at the crying porridge pot and shakes her head.) What am I suppose to do with you?

Porridge Pot: Well, if you are hungry just say, 'Boil, pot, boil, pot.'

(Porridge comes out and spreads all over. This can be mimed.)

Daisy: How wonderful, but how do I stop the porridge flowing?

Porridge Pot: Just say, 'Stop, pot! Stop, pot!'

Daisy: Stop, pot! Stop, pot! *(Daisy brings the pot home and shows her mother and they both eat until they are full.)*

Mother: This is wonderful. We should make some for the neighbours.

Daisy: Oh no, we should keep this as our own secret.

Storyteller 1: One day, the little girl went out playing with her friend Maisy.

Maisy: Let's go into the forest and play hide-and-seek. *(Maisy and Daisy skip off stage.)*

Storyteller 2: Her mother was feeling hungry and she got the porridge pot to boil.

Mother: Boil, pot! Boil, pot! *(Mother eats her porridge but she wants it to stop.)*

Mother: I am full now so halt, pot! Halt, pot!

Storyteller 1: The porridge pot kept boiling.

Storyteller 2: There was porridge all over the place. (*Mother jumps up on a chair.*)

Mother: Don't, pot! Don't, pot!

Storyteller 1: The porridge spread everywhere.

Mother: Please, pot! Please, pot!

Villager 1: What is going on here?

Villager 2: The streets are paved with porridge.

Villager 3: Come, everyone, let's fill ourselves up with porridge.

Villager 4: This is delicious. Yummy! (*The villagers start swimming through the porridge.*)

Villager 1: There is a porridge flood!

Villager 2: Help us!

Villager 3: We are drowning!

Villager 4: In porridge!

Mother: Oh dear, no, pot! No, pot! (*Daisy returns with Maisy. She looks confused and shocked.*)

Daisy: (*Shouts*) Stop, pot! Stop, pot!

(*Porridge pot stops boiling porridge.*)

Storyteller 1: The villagers had porridge for the rest of the winter.

Storyteller 2: They weren't hungry. (*Everybody is eating porridge and the porridge pot looks happy.*)

Storyteller 1: In the spring, the old woman came back from her travels.

Storyteller 2: She asked for her pot back.

Old Woman: Thanks for taking care of my magic porridge pot.

Daisy: I didn't take care of it. It took care of us.

The Stone Soup

Characters: Three storytellers, three travellers and six villagers.

Storyteller 1: A long, long time ago, a group of weary travellers came across a small village on the edge of a large forest. (*Three travellers enter the stage looking very tired and walking very slowly.*)

Traveller 1: I am so tired and hungry. (*He rubs his stomach.*)

Traveller 2: We have been walking for hours. Surely we will come across somewhere to eat and lay our heads down soon.

Traveller 3: Look over there. (*Points*) I see smoke; we must be near some houses.

Traveller 1: It is a little village.

Traveller 2: Someone is bound to let us in.

Traveller 3: I would do anything for a very large bowl of hot, warm soup.

Storyteller 2: As they walked quietly through the village, they noticed that the village was very quiet and it seemed deserted. (*They all look around carefully and slowly.*)

Traveller 1: No one seems to live here.

Traveller 2: I think we should put up our tent and go to sleep.

Traveller 3: Maybe we will find food in the morning. *(They mime putting up their tent.)*

Storyteller 3: They started to put up their tent.

Storyteller 1: Then suddenly, the door of a cottage creaked opened. *(Villager 1 enters stage followed by some of the other villagers.)*

Villager 1: What are you doing here?

Traveller 2: We have been travelling for days. We just want to have something warm to eat and a place to lay our heads.

Villager 2: We have had a long, cold winter and we do not have any food left.

Villager 3: We cannot even feed ourselves, never mind strangers.

Villager 4: We are so poor and hungry that we cannot give you anything, so you should be off. *(Shoos them away.)*

Traveller 3: We are going to make a hearty stone soup. If you wish, you can have some too as there will be plenty to share.

Storyteller 3: The villagers could not believe their luck.

Villager 5: I have never heard of stone soup. Does it taste nice?

Traveller 2: It is the most delicious soup that you will ever have tasted.

Traveller 1: It is hot and tasty, but we need some wood to make a fire.

Villager 6: We might have enough firewood between us to build a fire.

Villager 1: We could give you some wood in exchange for a bowl of stone soup.

Storyteller 1: They all shook hands on it. *(The villagers all collect firewood and bring it back to the travellers who make the fire.)*

Storyteller 2: It was not long before the travellers made a big fire from all the wood that the villagers gave them.

Storyteller 3: They placed a large, black cooking pot on the fire and filled it with water.

Storyteller 1: All the villagers and travellers stood by the fire. *(They are warming themselves and chatting to one another.)*

Villager 2: This is lovely and warm.

Villager 3: What a good idea we had to put our wood together.

Storyteller 2: One of the travellers opened his bag and took out the stone.

Villager 4: Is that it?

Villager 5: That just looks like an ordinary plain stone.

Traveller 3: This no ordinary stone. It is a special soup stone. *(Drops the stone into the water.)*

Traveller 2: (*Dips spoon into the soup.*) Mmmm.

Villagers: Is it good?

Traveller 2: It needs some salt.

Traveller 1: Do any of you have salt?

Villagers: No. (*Shaking their heads.*)

Traveller 3: What a pity; it is no good without salt. I will throw it away. (*Goes to throw it away.*)

Villager 6: Wait! I might be able to find some. (*Fetches some salt and puts it in the soup.*)

Traveller 2: Much better. The only thing is, it needs some parsley. Do you have some parsley?

Villagers: No. (*Shaking their heads.*)

Traveller 2: Oh, what a pity we have to throw it away. (*Goes to throw it away.*)

Villager 1: Wait! I might be able to find some. (*Fetches some parsley and puts it in the pot.*)

Traveller 2: Much better, the only thing we are missing is some carrots. Does anyone have carrots?

Villagers: No. (*Shaking their heads.*)

Traveller 3: What a pity the soup is no good; we have to throw it away.

Villager 2: Wait! I might be able to find some. (*Fetches a carrot and puts it in the pot.*)

Traveller 1: Does anyone have pepper?

Villager 3: I have. (*Fetches some pepper and throws it into the pot.*)

Traveller 3: What about onions? (*One of villagers gets some onions and puts them into the pot.*)

Storyteller 1: Before long, all types of food and seasoning went into the soup.

Storyteller 2: The soup was finally ready and everyone sat down and had a bowl.

Storyteller 3: After they had finished their delicious soup, they all danced and played music.

(*Music plays and everyone is dancing together.*)

Storyteller 1: The next day, the travellers packed up their tent and their belongings.

Villager 1: Stay for a little while longer!

Traveller 1: Unfortunately, we have to move on.

Traveller 2: Because we are travellers.

Traveller 3: (*Unwraps the stone and gives it to the villager.*) This is for you. It will only work if you cook together and everyone brings some food to put into the pot.

Storyteller 2: The travellers waved goodbye and set off.

(*Once out of the village, one of travellers bends down and picks up a large stone.*)

Travellers: You never know when we might need you.

The Pied Piper of Hamelin

Characters: Two narrators, mayor, town crier, two town councillors, four rats, four townspeople, four children, a shopkeeper and two soldiers.

Narrator 1: Once upon a time in a town in Germany called Hamelin...

Narrator 2: They had a big rat problem. One day, the mayor called a town meeting.

Townsperson 1: Our home is full of rats.

Townsperson 2: The town councillors should do something before this causes a plague.

Townsperson 3: There are more and more of them every day.

Shopkeeper: They have eaten all my supplies.

Townsperson 4: They have bitten my baby.

(Rats come scurrying onto the stage and scare the mayor and townspeople.)

Rats: *(Sing)* Rats, rats, rats. We fought the dogs and killed the cats, and bit the babies in the cradles, and ate the cheeses out of the vats, and licked the soup from the cooks' own ladles. Rats, rats, rats!

Mayor: I need to call the town councillors.

Town Crier: Hear ye! Hear ye! The meeting of the town councillors has commenced.

Town Councillor 1: We have to do something.

Town Councillor 2: We could set traps.

Town Councillor 1: They won't work; there are too many rats.

Town Councillor 2: I know! We could offer a reward to whoever can get rid of them.

Mayor: What a splendid idea. We could offer a thousand gold coins.

Town Crier: Hear ye! Hear ye! The mayor and the town councillors have offered a reward of a thousand gold coins to anyone who can get rid of the rats. *(He puts up some reward posters around the stage. Pied Piper enters and sees the posters and goes to see the mayor.)*

Pied Piper: I can get rid of the rats.

Mayor: You! But you are only a poor pied piper. How can YOU get rid of the rats?

Narrator 1: The pied piper began to play the most beautiful music. All the townspeople came to watch.

Rat 1: What beautiful music!

Rat 2: Where is it coming from?

Rat 3: Over there!

Rat 4: Let's follow it.

(All the rats follow the musician.)

Narrator 2: All the rats left the town and followed the pied piper. He walked into the river and all the rats followed him.

(All the rats are dragged downstream. They swim off the stage. Pied Piper comes out of the river and puts on his shoes. He goes to the mayor's office and knocks on his door.)

Town Crier: May I help you?

Pied Piper: I demand to see the mayor. *(Mayor comes to the door.)*

Mayor: I don't have the gold coins. Besides, the rats are gone and are not coming back so I'm not going to give you the money.

(All the townspeople come on stage and surround the mayor.)

Townspeople: Three cheers for the mayor. The rats are gone.

Mayor: Oh thank you, thank you so much. It was my pleasure.

Pied Piper: *(Gets angry)* But you didn't do anything! I got rid of the rats.

Mayor: *(Pushes him away)* All you did was play some music. Be off with you.

Pied Piper: Pay me or you will rue the day that you crossed me. My revenge will destroy this town.

Mayor: Be off with you. Soldiers, take him away.

(Soldiers escort him out of the town. Outside the town, children are playing. The pied piper plays his music.)

Pied Piper: Come with me, children.

Child 1: We love your music.

Child 2: Please keep playing.

Child 3: Let's follow the beautiful music.

Child 4: *(Falls over and picks himself up.)* Wait for me!

(Back in the town)

Townsperson 1: Mayor, please help us.

Shopkeeper: All the children have gone.

Mayor: This is the revenge of the pied piper.

Narrator 1: The children were never seen again. There were no longer any rats in Hamelin but there were also no longer any children.

Narrator 2: The moral of the story is always keep to your word.

The Little Red Hen

Characters: Six storytellers, the Little Red Hen, dog 1, dogs, cat 1, cats, goose 1, geese, duck 1, ducks *(you can have as many dogs, cats, ducks and geese as you want)*, **farmer and miller.**

(Stage Directions: Storytellers are on the left-side of the stage and the animals are all in a semi-circle in the centre of the stage.)

Storyteller 1: Once upon a time, there was a little red hen that lived on a farm.

Storyteller 2: She was always busy! *(She moves around the stage looking busy.)*

Storyteller 3: She spent all morning laying eggs for the farmer. *(The Little Red Hen bends down and lays eggs. Balloons can be used for the eggs.)*

Farmer: Chick chicken! Please lay an egg for my tea. *(The Farmer walks to the centre stage and talks to the Little Red Hen.)*

All Sing: Chick, chick, chick, chicken,

Chick, chick, chick, chick, chicken,

Lay a little egg for me!

Chick, chick, chick, chick, chicken,

I want one for my tea!

I haven't had an egg since Easter

69

And now it's half past three!

So chick, chick, chick, chick, chicken

Lay a little egg for me!

Storyteller 4: After the Little Red Hen laid her egg...

Storyteller 5: She found a grain of wheat.

Storyteller 6: She wanted to plant it in a field.

Red Hen: I think I'll ask my animal friends to help me. *(She moves towards the dogs.)* Dogs, dogs! Will you help me plant the wheat?

Dogs: Oh no, we will not help you. We are too busy burying our bones. *(They all make burying actions.)*

Dog 1: Get the ducks to help you. *(They all point to the ducks.)*

Red Hen: Ducks, ducks! Will you help me plant the wheat? *(Little Red Hen moves towards the ducks.)*

Ducks: Oh no, we will not help you. We are too busy swimming. *(They all make swimming actions.)*

Duck 1: Get the geese to help you. *(All the ducks point to the geese.)*

Red Hen: Geese, geese! Will you help me plant the wheat? *(She moves towards the geese.)*

Geese: Oh no, we will not help you. We are too busy sunbathing. *(All the geese are lying on the floor enjoying the sun and rubbing lotion on themselves.)*

Goose 1: Get the cats to help you. *(All geese point towards the cats.)*

Red Hen: Cats, cats! Will you help me plant the wheat?

Cats: Oh no, we will not help you. We are too busy licking our paws. *(Cats lick their paws.)*

Cat 1: Plant it yourself.

Storyteller 6: No one would help the Little Red Hen, so she planted it herself. *(Red Hen, centre stage, mimes planting the wheat.)*

Storyteller 1: The sun and the rain helped the wheat to grow.

Storyteller 2: Soon, the wheat was tall and yellow and needed to be cut.

Red Hen: I think I'll ask my animal friends to help me. Dogs, dogs! Will you help me cut the wheat? *(She moves towards the dogs.)*

Dogs: Oh no, we will not help you. We are too busy burying our bones. *(The dogs mime burying their bones.)*

Dog 1: Get the ducks to help you. *(Dogs point at the ducks.)*

Red Hen: Ducks, ducks! Will you help me cut the wheat?

Ducks: Oh no, we will not help you. We are too busy swimming.

Duck 1: Get the geese to help you. *(All the ducks point to the geese.)*

Red Hen: Geese, geese! Will you help me cut the wheat?

Geese: Oh no, we will not help you. We are too busy sunbathing.

Goose 1: Get the cats to help you. (*All geese point to the cats.*)

Red Hen: Cats, cats! Will you help me cut the wheat?

Cats: Oh no, we will not help you. We are too busy washing our faces.

Cat 1: Plant it yourself.

Storyteller 3: So the Little Red Hen cut the wheat herself.

Storyteller 4: She took the wheat to the miller.

Storyteller 5: The miller turned the wheat into flour.

Miller: (*Gives Little Red Hen the bag of flour.*) Here's your flour to make bread and cakes.

Storyteller 6: The little red hen thanked the miller.

Storyteller 1: She made bread and cakes.

Red Hen: Who will help me eat the bread?

All animals: We will!

Red Hen: Oh no, I will eat it myself. If you want to eat the food what will you do next time?

All: We will share the work.

Storytellers: THE END!

All sing: Chick, chick, chick, and chicken.

Chick, chick, chick, chick, chicken,

Lay a little egg for me!

Chick, chick, chick, chick, chicken,

I want one for my tea!

I haven't had an egg since Easter

And now it's half past three!

So chick, chick, chick, chick, chicken

Lay a little egg for me!

Julie Meighan

The Gingerbread Man

Characters: Gingerbread Man, three storytellers, old woman, old man, cow, horse, dog, two bears and a fox.

(Stage Directions: Three storytellers stand on the left side of the stage. Old woman is sitting on a chair knitting or reading a book and Old Man is digging up vegetables on the right side of stage. The rest of the animals can be back stage or standing quietly in a semicircle.)

Storyteller 1: Once upon a time, a little old woman and a little old man lived in a little old house. One day, the little old woman decided to make a gingerbread man.

Old Woman: I think I will make gingerbread for the old man's tea. He will love that. *(She gets up from the chair and goes to centre stage. She mimes making the gingerbread and putting it in the oven as Storyteller 2 speaks.)*

Storyteller 2: She cut the Gingerbread Man out of dough. She gave him chocolate drops for eyes and a piece of lemon for his mouth. Then she put him in the oven to bake. After a while, she said to herself...

Old Woman: That Gingerbread Man must be ready by now. *(She mimes looking into the oven, etc.)*

Storyteller 3: She opened the oven door. UP jumped the Gingerbread Man, and away he ran, out the front door! *(Gingerbread Man jumps out from the oven.)*

Gingerbread Man: Hello, I am the Gingerbread Man.

74

Old Man: Don't run away. I want you for my tea. *(He puts his hand up to try and stop the Gingerbread Man.)*

Gingerbread Man: Run, run, as fast as you can. You can't catch me. I'm the Gingerbread Man!

Storyteller 3: The little old woman and the little old man ran, but they couldn't catch the Gingerbread Man. *(They run after him, running around the stage in a circle. Old Man and Old Woman get tired, so they stop.)*

Storyteller 1: The Gingerbread Man ran past the cow grazing in the field. *(Cow comes out onto the stage.)*

Cow: Moo! Moo! Stop! Stop! Gingerbread Man, I want to eat you.

Gingerbread Man: Run, run, as fast as you can. You can't catch me. I'm the Gingerbread Man! *(Cow chases him but can't catch him, so she stops and either goes back to her original position or goes off stage.)*

Storyteller 2: The cow ran, but she couldn't catch the Gingerbread Man. Then he met a horse drinking at the well. *(Horse comes out onto the stage.)*

Horse: Neigh! Neigh! Stop! Stop! Gingerbread Man, I want to eat you.

Gingerbread Man: Run, run, as fast as you can. You can't catch me. I'm the Gingerbread Man! *(Horse chases him but can't catch him so he stops.)*

Storyteller 3: The horse ran, but she couldn't catch the Gingerbread Man. Then he met a dog playing in the field. *(Dog comes out onto the stage.)*

Dog: Woof! Woof! Stop! Stop! Gingerbread Man, I want to eat you.

Gingerbread Man: Run, run, as fast as you can. You can't catch me. I'm the Gingerbread Man! *(Dog chases him but he gets tired and stops. Dog is panting.)*

Storyteller 1: He ran between two bears having a picnic.

Bears: Growl! Growl! Stop! Stop! Gingerbread Man, we want to eat you.

Gingerbread Man: Run, run, as fast as you can. You can't catch me. I'm the Gingerbread Man! *(Bears chase the Gingerbread Man but they get tired and have to stop.)*

Storyteller 2: The bears jumped up and ran after him. They ran and ran, but they couldn't catch that Gingerbread Man!

Storyteller 3: Soon, the Gingerbread Man came to a river and started to cry. *(Gingerbread Man cries and Fox creeps up behind him.)* He saw a fox.

Fox: Why are you crying, Gingerbread Man?

Gingerbread Man: I've run away from an old woman, an old man, a cow, a horse, a dog and two picnicking bears, and I can run away from you!

Fox: If you don't get across this river quickly, the old woman, the old man, the cow, the horse, the dog and the two picnicking bears will surely catch you. Hop on my tail and I'll carry you across. *(Fox points to his tail.)*

Storyteller 2: The Gingerbread Man saw that he had no time to lose because the old woman, the old man, the cow, the horse, the dog and the two picnicking bears were very close behind him. He quickly hopped onto the fox's tail. (*Gingerbread Man mimes getting onto the fox's tail. He holds on to his back and fox mimes swimming.*)

Fox: The water's deep; climb up on my back so you won't get wet. Oh! The water's even deeper! Climb up on my head so you won't get wet! (*Gingerbread Man holds onto Fox's back and he jumps in front. Then Fox bends down, so his head is touching Gingerbread Man's back.*)

Storyteller 3: And the Gingerbread Man did as the fox told him.

Fox: It's too deep! Climb onto my nose so you won't get wet! (*The gingerbread man's back touches the fox's nose.*)

Storyteller 1: And the Gingerbread Man did that but then, with a flick of his head, the Fox tossed the Gingerbread Man into the air and opened his mouth, but the Gingerbread Man jumped to the other side of the river.

Gingerbread Man: (*To everyone*) Run, run, as fast as you can. You can't catch me. I'm the Gingerbread Man!

(*All the other characters are on the other side of the stage/river and they start to cry.*)

The Enormous Turnip

Characters: Three storytellers, old man, old woman, boy, girl, dog, cat and mouse.

(Stage Directions: storytellers on stage left and the old man in the centre. All the other characters are in a line off-stage or they can be on stage, with each character miming doing their own thing.)

Storyteller 1: Once upon a time, there lived a little old man.

Storyteller 2: One day, he planted a turnip seed in his garden. *(Old man plants his seed.)*

Old Man: This turnip is going to be very big and very sweet. *(Looks at the audience.)*

Storyteller 3: The turnip grew and grew.

Old Man: I think it is time to dig up the turnip. *(Old man mimes trying to pull it up.)*

Storyteller 1: He pulled and pulled, but he couldn't pull up the turnip.

Old Man: I know, I will ask my wife to help me. Wife! Wife! Please help me to pull up the turnip. *(Wife holds on to him at the waist and they try pulling up the turnip.)*

Storyteller 2: His wife came and helped him.

Storyteller 3: They pulled and pulled, but they couldn't pull up the turnip.

Wife: I know, I will ask the boy to help us. Boy! Boy! Please help us to pull up the turnip. *(She calls for the boy and the boy comes to help them.)*

Storyteller 1: The boy came and helped them. *(The boy holds on to her at the waist.)*

Storyteller 2: They pulled and pulled, but they couldn't pull up the turnip.

Boy: I know, I will ask the girl to help us. Girl! Girl! Please help us to pull up the turnip. *(He calls for the girl and the girl comes to help them.)*

Storyteller 3: The girl came and helped them. *(The girl holds on to him at the waist.)*

Storyteller 1: They pulled and pulled but they couldn't pull up the turnip.

Girl: I know, I will ask the dog to help us. Dog! Dog! Please help us to pull up the turnip. *(She calls for the dog and the dog comes to help her.)*

Storyteller 2: The dog came and helped them. *(The dog holds on to her at the waist.)*

Storyteller 3: They pulled and pulled but they couldn't pull up the turnip.

Dog: I know, I will ask the cat to help us. Cat! Cat! Please help us to pull up the turnip. *(He calls for the cat and the cat comes to help them.)*

Storyteller 1: The cat came and helped them. *(The cat holds on to him at the waist.)*

Storyteller 2: They pulled and pulled, but they couldn't pull up the turnip.

Cat: I know, I will ask the mouse to help us. Mouse! Mouse! Please help us to pull up the turnip. *(She calls for the mouse and the mouse comes to help them.)*

Storyteller 3: The mouse came and helped them. *(The mouse holds onto her at the waist.)*

Storyteller 1: They pulled and pulled and then suddenly they pulled up the turnip. *(They all fall over.)*

Storyteller 2: Everyone was very happy and they all thanked the mouse. *(Everyone shakes hands with the mouse.)*

Storyteller 3: Everyone had turnip soup for dinner. *(The wife mimes giving each one of them a bowl of soup and they mime drinking it.)*

Chicken Licken

Characters: Three storytellers, Chicken-Licken, Cockey-Lockey, Ducky-Lucky, Goosey-Loosey, Turkey-Lurkey and Foxy-Loxy.

(Stage Directions: Chicken-Licken is moving around the centre stage, miming picking up corn. All the other animals are either off stage or on the stage miming doing different things. Storytellers are stage left.)

Storyteller 1: One summer's day, Chicken-Licken was busy picking up corn in the barnyard. *(Chicken Licken is moving around the stage, miming picking up corn.)*

Storyteller 2: When all of a sudden, an acorn from the big oak tree fell down and hit her right on the top of her head. Kerrrr flop.

Storyteller 3: She got a terrible fright.

Chicken-Licken: Oh! The sky is falling! The sky is falling! I am going to tell the king!

Storyteller 1: And away she went, to tell the king the sky was falling down. After a while, she came to Cockey-Lockey. *(Cockey-Lockey walks towards Chicken-Licken who is in the centre of the stage.)*

Cockey-Lockey: Where are you going, Chicken-Licken?

Chicken-Licken: Oh, Cockey-Lockey. The sky is falling! I am going to tell the king.

Cockey-Lockey: I will go with you! *(They walk in a circle around the stage and they come back to the centre stage where they see Ducky-Lucky.)*

Storyteller 2: They went on and on and on. After a time, they met Ducky-Lucky.

Ducky-Lucky: Where are you going, Chicken-Licken and Cockey-Lockey?

Chicken-Licken/Cockey-Lockey: Oh, Ducky-Lucky! The sky is falling! We are going to tell the king!

Ducky-Lucky: Wait! I will go with you. *(They walk in a circle around the stage and they come back to the centre stage where they see Goosey-Loosey.)*

Storyteller 3: And they hurried off. They went on and on and on! Soon they came to Goosey-Loosey.

Goosey: Hey, where are you two going?

Chicken/Cockey/ Ducky: Oh, Goosey-Loosey! The sky is falling! We are going to tell the king.

Goosey: Then I will go with you! *(They walk in a circle around the stage and they come back to the centre stage where they meet Turkey-Lurkey.)*

Storyteller 3: Before long, they came to Turkey-Lurkey.

Turkey: Where are you all going in such a rush?

All: Oh, Turkey-Lurkey. The sky is falling! We are going to tell the king.

Turkey: Well, hey, wait for me! I will go with you. *(They walk in a circle around the stage and they come back to the centre stage where they see the fox.)*

Storyteller 1: They went on and on and on. After a while they came to Foxy-Loxy.

Foxy: Say, where are you all going?

All: Foxy-Loxy! Foxy-Loxy! The sky is falling! We are going to tell the king.

Foxy: Well, I know a short cut to the king's palace. Follow me.

Turkey: Oh, great! He knows a short cut to the king's palace!

Storytellers: They went on and on and on. Then they came to Foxy-Loxy's house. *(They all follow Foxy-Loxy, walking in a straight line.)*

Foxy: This is the short cut to the palace. I'll go in first and then you follow me, one-by-one. *(One-by-one they go into the den. The den can be off-stage in the front or behind stage.)*

Storytellers: In went Turkey-Lurkey. Sssssnap! Off went Turkey-Lurkey's head. In went Goosey-Loosey. Kerrrr-POP! Off went Goosey-Loosey's head. In went Ducky-Lucky. Kerrrr-unch! Off went Ducky-Lucky's head. In went Cocky-Lockey. *(Chicken-Licken looks into the den and sees what is happening.)*

Cockey: *(Excitedly)* Go Home, Chicken-Licken! Go Home!

Storyteller 1: Can you guess what happened next? *(Pause)* Kerrrrr-Aaaack! Off went Cockey-Lockey's head.

Storyteller 2: Chicken-Licken ran home. (*Chicken-Licken runs really fast around the stage, looking scared.*) She did not tell the king that the sky was falling.

Storyteller 3: And since that day, the others have never been seen again. And the poor king has never been told that the sky is falling down!

CPSIA information can be obtained
at www.ICGtesting.com
Printed in the USA
BVHW042358190423
662662BV00001B/1